FIGHTING FORCES IN THE AIR

NIGHTHAWK F-117A

LYNN STONE

Rourke
Publishing LLC
Vero Beach, Florida 32964

www.rourkepublishing.com

PHOTO CREDITS: All photos courtesy of the U.S. Air Force

Title page: *The U.S. Air Force has about 50 Nighthawks in service.*

Editor: Frank Sloan

Library of Congress Cataloging-in-Publication Data

Stone, Lynn M.
  Nighthawk F-117A / Lynn M. Stone.
     p. cm. -- (Fighting forces in the air)
  Includes bibliographical references and index.
  ISBN 1-59515-183-4 (hardcover)
  1. F-117 (Jet fighter plane) I. Title. II. Series: Stone, Lynn M. Fighting forces in the air.
  UG1242.F5S79 2004
  623.74'63--dc22

                                    2004011746

Printed in the USA

CG/CG

TABLE OF CONTENTS

THE F-117A NIGHTHAWK

The twin-engine F-117A Nighthawk of the United States Air Force was the world's first combat-ready **stealth** aircraft. The first Nighthawks were operational—ready for Air Force missions—in 1983.

The "F" designation by the Air Force classifies the Nighthawk as a fighter, but it has been used largely as an air-to-surface attack plane. Its greatest value has been in making precision attacks on heavily guarded ground targets.

Trailing a parachute to slow its landing, a ▶
Nighthawk touches onto the runway.

▲
Like a giant moth, an F-117 flies over the Persian Gulf during Operation Iraqi Freedom.

The F-117A is an unusual looking plane. Seen from above, it looks like a giant sphinx moth with folded wings. It has been nicknamed Frisbee, because of its broad, flat profile, and Wobblin' Goblin'. The Air Force has been mum, but some air experts think the Nighthawk has a tendency to wobble in certain flight conditions.

F-117A
CHARACTERISTICS

FUNCTION: FIGHTER/ATTACK

BUILDER: LOCKHEED
AERONAUTICAL SYSTEMS
COMPANY

POWER SOURCE: TWO GENERAL
ELECTRIC F404 NON-
AFTERBURNING ENGINES

THRUST: CLASSIFIED (SECRET)

LENGTH: 63 FEET, 9 INCHES
(19.4 M)

HEIGHT: 12 FEET, 9.5 INCHES
(3.9 M)

WINGSPAN: 43 FEET, 4 INCHES
(13.2 M)

SPEED: HIGH SUBSONIC (LESS
THAN THE SPEED OF SOUND)

CEILING: CLASSIFIED (SECRET)

WEIGHT: 52,500 POUNDS
(23,625 KG)

RANGE: UNLIMITED WITH AIR
REFUELING

CREW: ONE

DATE DEPLOYED: 1982

Air Force fighters like the F-15 Eagle and F-16 Fighting Falcon are highly **maneuverable** speed burners. Both can fly at or beyond **Mach** 2, which is twice the speed of sound. The Nighthawk flies at **subsonic** speeds—speeds slower than sound travels. The Nighthawk is also less maneuverable than true air-to-air fighters.

And because stealth design did away with certain conventional aircraft features, like wing flaps to slow descent, the Nighthawk lands at about 185 miles per hour (296 km/h). That is an unusually fast landing speed, so the F-117A employs a drag parachute. As the airplane touches down, the parachute slows its speed.

FACT FILE ★

THE NIGHTHAWK IS ABOUT THE SAME SIZE AS THE F-15, BUT THE F-117A IS A MUCH DIFFERENT AIRPLANE IN PURPOSE, APPEARANCE, HANDLING, AND MANEUVERABILITY.

The Nighthawk is most unusual, though, because of its stealth **capability.** Because it wanted to guard stealth knowledge, the Air Force kept the Nighthawk secret for several years. By flying the Nighthawk always at night, the Air Force kept the public in the dark about the F-117A. Secrecy still surrounds some of the Nighthawk's stealth and flying capabilities. Nevertheless, neither the airplane nor its stealth is quite the mystery it once was.

▲

An F-117A makes a parachute-assisted landing in the Middle East after a combat mission in March, 2003.

Normally painted black and used for night flight, this Nighthawk is being painted gray for possible daytime use.

Stealth is the name given to aircraft that have an extremely small "radar print." A small radar print does not happen by chance. Even a small plane can have a rather large radar print. Making an airplane with stealth technology to achieve a small radar print takes a great deal of research and design.

▲
The low profile of the F-117A helps reduce its radar imprint.

Stealth is employed to outfox radar. Radar systems are used by nations all over the world to detect flying objects. Radar works on the principle of sending sound waves into the air. When the waves strike a flying object, they bounce back to the radar site. The radar system uses the signals to identify the flying object, its distance, and its speed, often with great accuracy.

Once radar detects a flying plane, the plane no longer has the advantage of surprise. Having been "discovered," even if it can't be seen by the naked eye, it is now at the risk of air defenses, such as surface-to-air missiles (SAMs). And for most airplanes, being detected by ground radar is not a matter of *if*. It is a matter of *when*. That is because the radar print of most airplanes is obvious. After all, even *birds* turn up on radar screens.

The lean, straight lines of an F-117A are clear as it streaks over New Mexico on a training flight.

▲
Flat surfaces of the Nighthawk add to its stealth.

By making the Nighthawk "stealthy," its builders reduced its radar print to almost zero. The surfaces and edges of the Nighthawk airframe are designed to reflect enemy radar into narrow beam signals. The Nighthawk is covered with small, flat surfaces that reflect radar signals in many directions, rather than neatly back to the ground detector. In addition, the doors and opening panels on the F-117A have saw-toothed edges that also reflect radar. A flying F-117A has such a sleek, saucer-like profile that it can be difficult to see even with the naked eye.

FACT FILE ★

THE OUTER SURFACE OF THE AIRCRAFT IS COATED WITH A SPECIAL—AND SECRET—MATERIAL THAT ABSORBS RADAR.

One pilot flies the F-117A.

CHAPTER TWO

FLYING THE F-117A

The Nighthawk is flown by a single pilot. The pilot's job is made easier by advanced **avionics**. Avionics are the electronic devices that provide information and pilot guidance in an aircraft. The Nighthawk has, for instance, **navigation** and attack avionics that are blended together. This arrangement improves the plane's ability to carry out its mission. It also lightens the pilot's workload.

Before a mission, data is downloaded into an IBM AP-102 mission control computer. The computer matches the mission data with navigation and flight controls. That provides the pilot with a fully automated flight control option.

FACT FILE ★

THE COMPUTER, IN EFFECT, CAN FLY THE PLANE TO THE ATTACK SITE, WHERE THE PILOT RETAKES CONTROL OF THE AIRCRAFT FOR RELEASING WEAPONS.

Much of the information produced by Nighthawk avionics appears on a cockpit HUD—a mounted display screen that allows the pilot to keep his or her head up. The cockpit also has a full-color moving map.

Outside the plane are **infrared** sensors. One of their jobs is to sense for the heat trail that an enemy missile would create. A large video screen on the flight deck displays images from those sensors.

For reasons related to stealth, the F-117A does not rely on its own radar to navigate or target. Instead, it uses infrared systems, both forward-looking (FLIR) and downward-looking (DLIR).

▲

High-tech flight systems in the Nighthawk make it a deadly night fighter and attack plane.

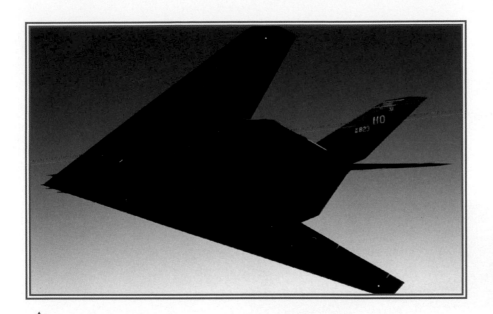

▲

The exhaust system of the Nighthawk is designed to reduce the airplane's heat trail.

To help avoid attack, the F-117A has a special exhaust system that reduces its heat trail. Narrow-slot "platypus" exhausts are surrounded by tiles that absorb heat. They further reduce the chance of detection by heat-seeking weapons. The plane's two large tail fins slant slightly outward. They, too, help break up any radar or infrared data that enemy detectors might collect from the F-117A's engine exhaust.

Like most other modern military aircraft, the F-117A can be refueled in mid-air by air tanker planes. Nighthawks refueled in mid-air hold the record for the longest single-seat fighter flight—18.5 hours.

▲

An F-117A Nighthawk is refueled in mid-air.

CHAPTER THREE

FIREPOWER

The Nighthawk can carry a variety of weapons for air-to-surface strikes in its enclosed weapons **bay**. Nighthawks do not carry additional weapons on their wings, as many fighters do. Wing weapons would create **drag**, break up the Nighthawk's sleek silhouette, and make it unstealthy.

▲

Weapons aboard, Nighthawks line up for a combat mission in the Middle East.

For air-to-surface attack, a Nighthawk can carry AGM-65 Maverick and AGM-88 HARM missiles. The aircraft can also carry low-level laser-guided bombs, such as the BLU-109B. Each of the F-117A's bombs may weigh 2,000 pounds (907 kg).

▲

Combat-ready, a trio of stealth aircraft flies on a mission. A B-2 bomber (center) leads a pair of F-117As.

In 2004, a U.S. Air Force test pilot made the first-ever release of a JDAM weapon from an F-117A.

Among the newest weapons carried by Nighthawks are JDAM (Joint Direct Attack Munitions) bombs. JDAMs are "smart" bombs. Their flight is controlled by satellite GPS (Global Positioning System) and computer commands. Three movable fins, wired for computer command, can direct the bomb's path so that it can strike a specific target.

COMING OF AGE

CHAPTER FOUR

The U.S. Air Force wanted an airplane that could attack important targets—without being detected. Planning for an American stealth fighter began in the 1970s in complete secrecy. A test model called *Have Blue* eventually evolved into the F-117A Nighthawk. In 1978 the Air Force decided to have the Lockheed Martin Company produce the Nighthawk. By June, 1981, the Nighthawk had completed its first test flights. By 1990, Lockheed Martin had delivered the last of 59 Nighthawks for the Air Force.

▲

The first Nighthawks were delivered to the Air Force in 1982.

The Nighthawk was first used in combat during the United States' brief invasion of Panama in 1989. During Operation Desert Storm in 1991, Nighthawks flew about 1,300 sorties. Because of stealth capability, they were the only airplanes used to bomb specific targets in downtown Baghdad. In Operation Iraqi Freedom, F-117As led the first air strikes over Iraq in March, 2003. Twelve F-117As were deployed in Iraq.

An F-117A lifts off from Aviano Air Base, Italy, for a mission over Kosovo during the United Nations-led Operation Allied Force in 1999.

FLYING INTO THE FUTURE

Upgrades in the F-117A's avionics and weaponry will keep it flying for several more years in the Air Force arsenal. Planners are also discovering cheaper, more efficient methods to keep the F-117As coated with radar-absorbent material. Robots have helped trim the time and cost of manually repainting the planes. Eventually, faster and even better stealth fighters will replace the Air Force's 52 active Nighthawks.

Plans are for the F-117A to continue flying for the Air Force until at least 2018.

Glossary

avionics (AY vee ON iks) — the electronic systems and devices used in aviation

bay (BAY) — a chamber or hold for storing weapons in an aircraft body

capability (KAY puh BIL it ee) — the ability to do something; being capable of

drag (DRAG) — the friction that results from air passing along a moving surface

infrared (IN fruh RED) — (also known as *thermal radiation* or *infrared rays*) the invisible-to-the-naked-eye energy rays given off by any warm object, such as a human being, battle tank, or airplane; invisible heat rays that can be detected by special instruments

Mach (MAWK) — a high speed expressed by a Mach number; Mach 1 is the speed of sound

maneuverable (muh NYUV uh ruh bul) — able to move an object for a specific purpose

navigation (NAV uh GAY shun) — the process of direction-finding

stealth (STELTH) — the technology and various strategies used to make an aircraft invisible to radar detection

subsonic (SUB SON ik) — any speed below the speed of sound

INDEX

FURTHER READING

Berliner, Don. *Stealth Fighters and Bombers.*
   Enslow, 2001
Graham, Ian. *Attack Fighters.* Heinemann Library,
   2003
Reavis, Tracey. *Stealth Jet Fighter: The F-117A.*
   Scholastic, 2000

WEBSITES TO VISIT

http://www.af.mil/factsheets
http://www.fas.org/man/dod-101/sys/ac/f-117.htm

ABOUT THE AUTHOR

Lynn M. Stone is the author of more than 400 children's books. He is a talented natural history photographer as well. Lynn, a former teacher, travels worldwide to photograph wildlife in its natural habitat.